For Gabi —G. S.

For Lori —S. S.

HarperCollins Children's Books, a division of HarperCollins Publishers, 195 Broadway, New York, NY 10007
HarperCollins Publishers, Macken House, 39/40 Mayor Street Upper, Dublin 1, D01 C9W8, Ireland

Clarion Books is an imprint of HarperCollins Publishers.

Gifts from Crows

harpercollins.com

Library of Congress Control Number: 2026930749
ISBN 978-0-06-323758-2

The artist used watercolor, gouache, and ink with digital adjustments to create the illustrations for this book.
Typography by Chelsea C. Donaldson

26 27 28 29 30 RTLO 10 9 8 7 6 5 4 3 2 1

First Edition

Gifts from Crows

written by Gideon Sterer

illustrated by Shadra Strickland

CLARION
BOOKS
An Imprint of HarperCollinsPublishers

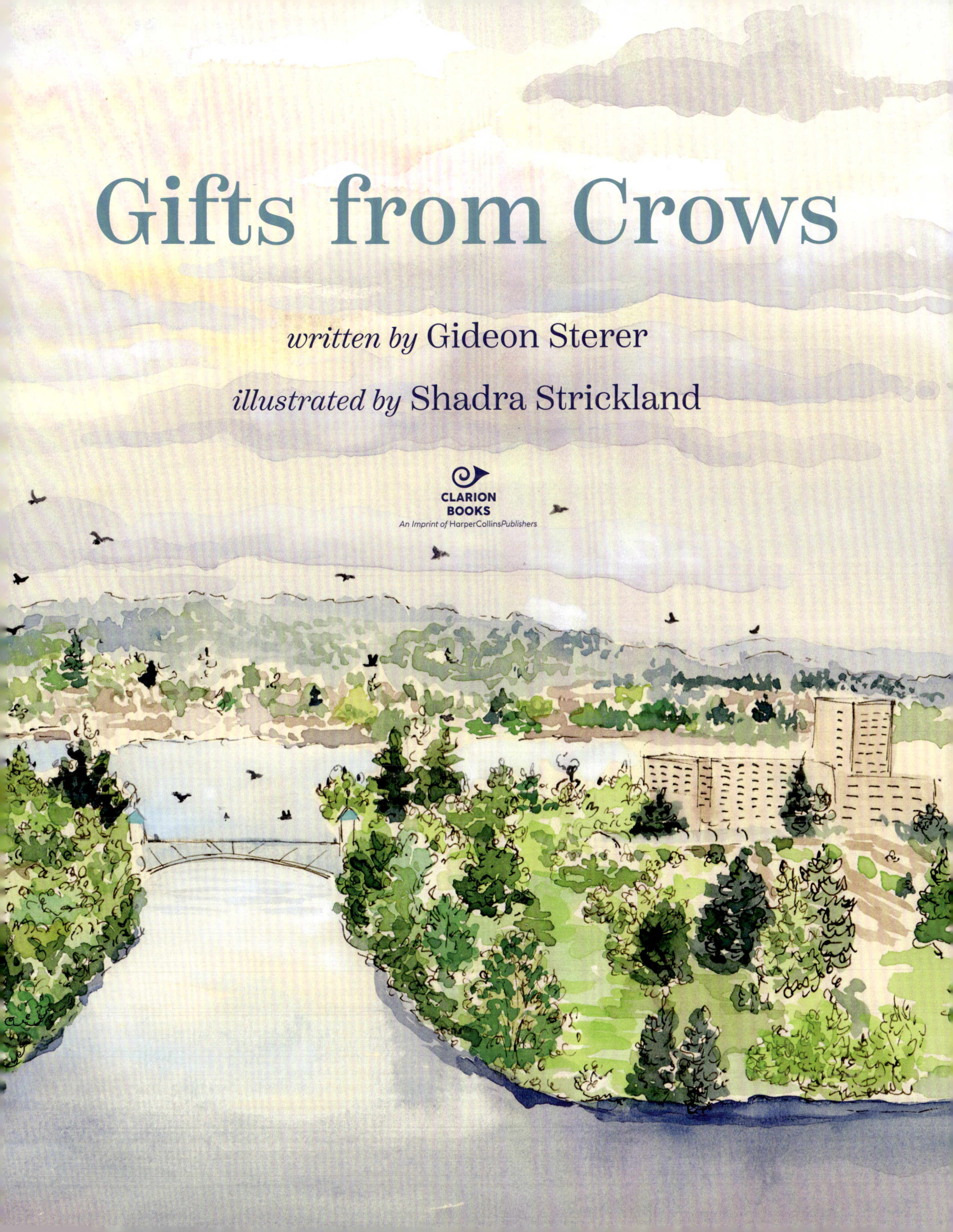

Not long ago, beyond the Puget Sound,
where the mountains meet the sea,
lived a girl named Gabi.

Her street was lined with tall trees and big yards,
and the sounds of birds were common.

Curious and kind, Gabi was four,
and like many her age,
she had a habit of dropping things.

This or that would fall to the ground and get left behind,
and much of the time it was food.

On it went like this,
and the family rarely noticed . . .

but someone else did.

What do you know about the crow?

For thousands of years, crows have lived beside us
in all corners of the world.
For thousands of years, humans have told stories of crows—
many of them sinister and strange.
Some considered crows to be ghosts or demons,
bringers of plague or bad luck,
or tricksters and thieves.

In ancient China, it was believed ten
crows carried the sun.

In ancient Rome, crows were thought to bring rain.
Others believed crows could predict the future
or deliver messages in dreams.

Every culture seems to have an opinion about crows.
But does that make any of it *true*?
Whatever the differences,
there was one thing humans agreed on. . . .

Crows are clever.

Clever enough, certainly, to spot a free meal.

Over time, as she grew, Gabi kept dropping food.

And over time, ever watchful, the crows would swoop and gobble it up.

Soon, whenever Gabi appeared, crows cawed from above, alerting family and friends.

They were *communicating.*

They were talking *about her.*

Which is no surprise . . .

. . . because crows are brilliant.

Compared to the size of their bodies, crows have some of the biggest brains on Earth.

One of the smartest animals on the planet, crows play games like tug-of-war and tag; they slide, snowboard, and play pranks.

They hang upside down and roll down hills. In short, they like to have fun.

Crows can also solve complex puzzles, mimic human voices, change accents, and make and use their own tools. In Sweden, crows pull up ice fishing lines and steal fish!

Across the world, crows have even learned how to read traffic lights, dropping food that needs cracking—like clams or nuts—in front of cars. Soon . . .

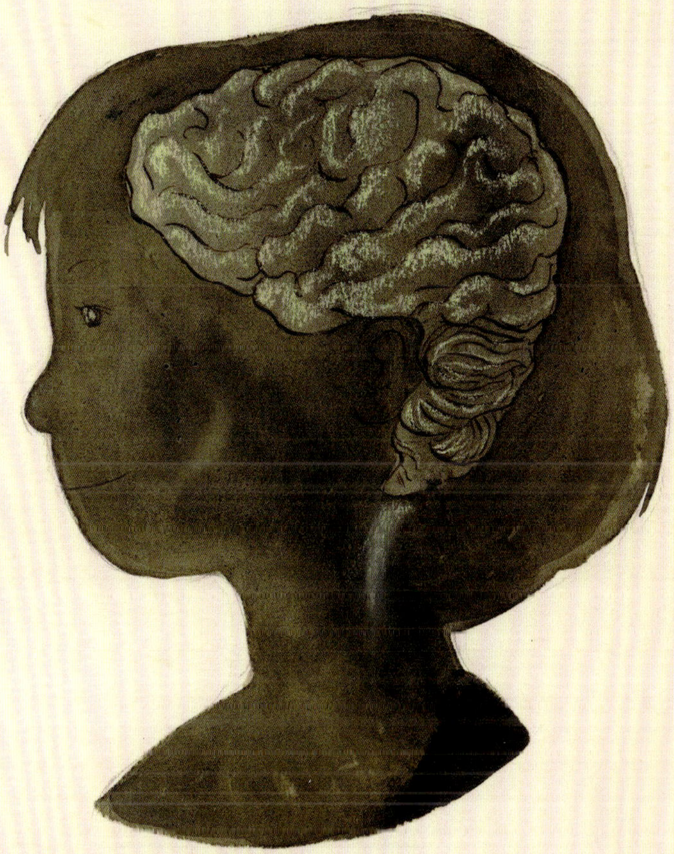

CRUNCH.

When the light turns red, dinner is served.

Crows can recognize human faces, and if a person is mean to them, they (and their children) won't forget for *generations.*

But if a person is kind . . .

As Gabi got older, soon she could recognize *their* faces too.

As they hopped and followed her to the school bus,
Gabi gave the crows nicknames like

Babyface

Spikey

and *Spacecraft*

and always shared her lunch.

Like people, each had a different personality, it seemed.

At school, Gabi thought about the crows.
And every day, when she returned home . . .

it was clear they thought about her too.

To Gabi, the crows were more than just birds.
They were family, and they were friends.

Which is no surprise because . . .

. . . crows are among the most social animals on Earth.

Often hundreds and even thousands will sleep together in roosts, finding safety and comfort in numbers.

Even after young crows mature, many will stay around the nest to lend a hand and help their parents raise new siblings.

Many crows mate for life.

Crows take turns as sentinels and lookouts, alerting the community to danger.

Crows have been known to feed their elderly and even wait for others before eating.

Astonishingly, it would seem crows even hold their own type of funeral.

To be a crow is to be part of a great family.

For two years Gabi had fed the crows,
and now she was six.
For two years she had grown close with crows young and old.
So why not, her family thought, set up a permanent feeding station
for her friends?

Every day, in her backyard, Gabi and her brother filled a birdbath
with fresh water and scattered peanuts and dog food.
You can imagine what the crows thought of that!

This went on for weeks, until . . .
one day, something strange appeared at the edge of the watering dish.

The rock was blue and gray and smooth,
and it had not come from the yard.

Neither Gabi nor her brother had put it there.

Someone else had.

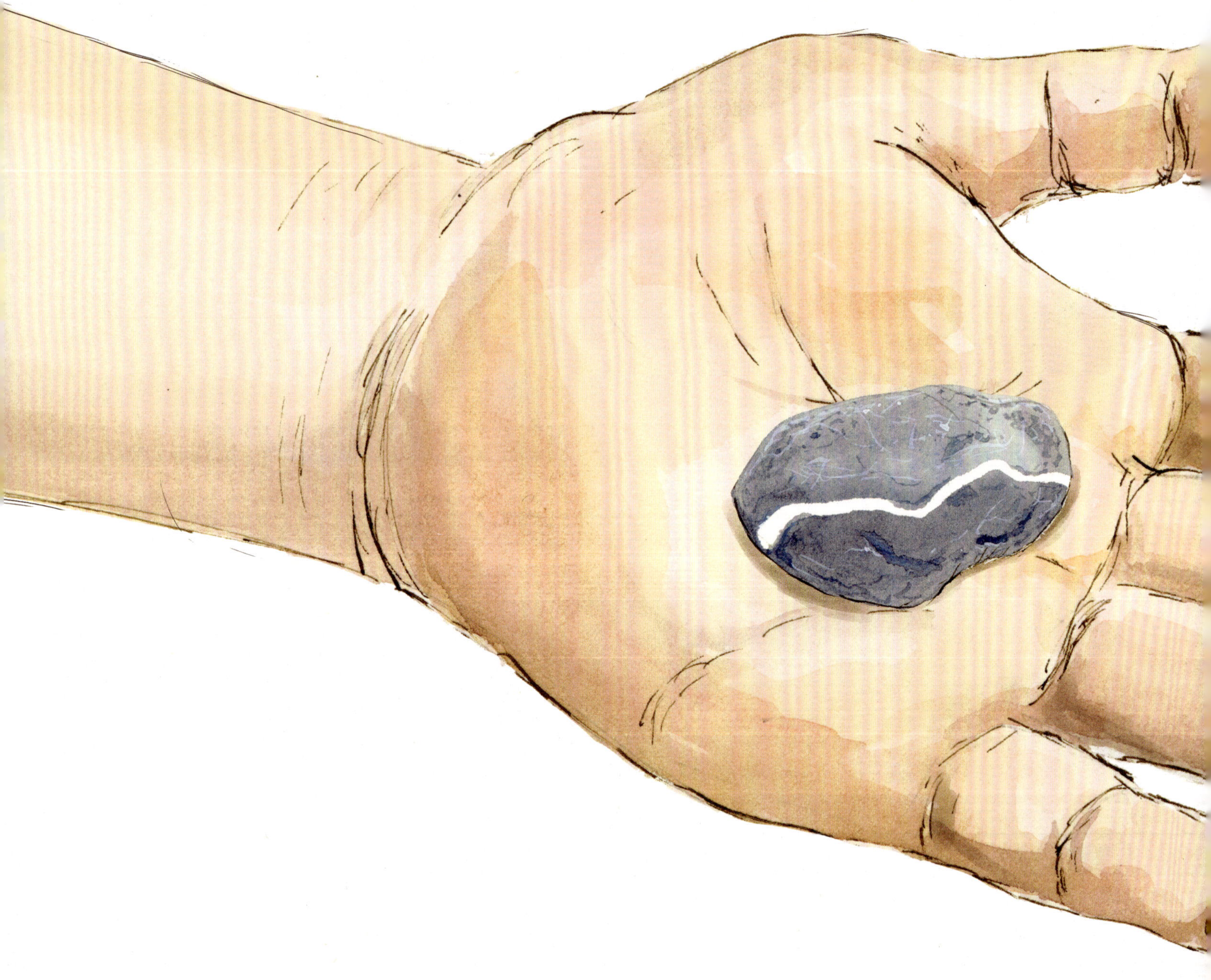

But why?

A few days later, another object arrived.

Then another.
        And another.
                And another.

There were paper clips,
Legos,
earrings,
buttons,
screws,
small pieces of stained glass—
even a pearl-colored heart.

FEBRUA
AU

Kraa!

By now, there was no mistaking who had brought them.

Were the crows saying *thank you*?
Indeed, the objects were gifts!

To Gabi, each was more precious than gold,
and all were labeled and stored.

For months,
then years,
the feathered friends visited her every morning.

Word spread of Gabi's generosity, and new birds, from near and far,
joined the daily feast.

So Gabi's collection of treasures grew

and grew

and grew.

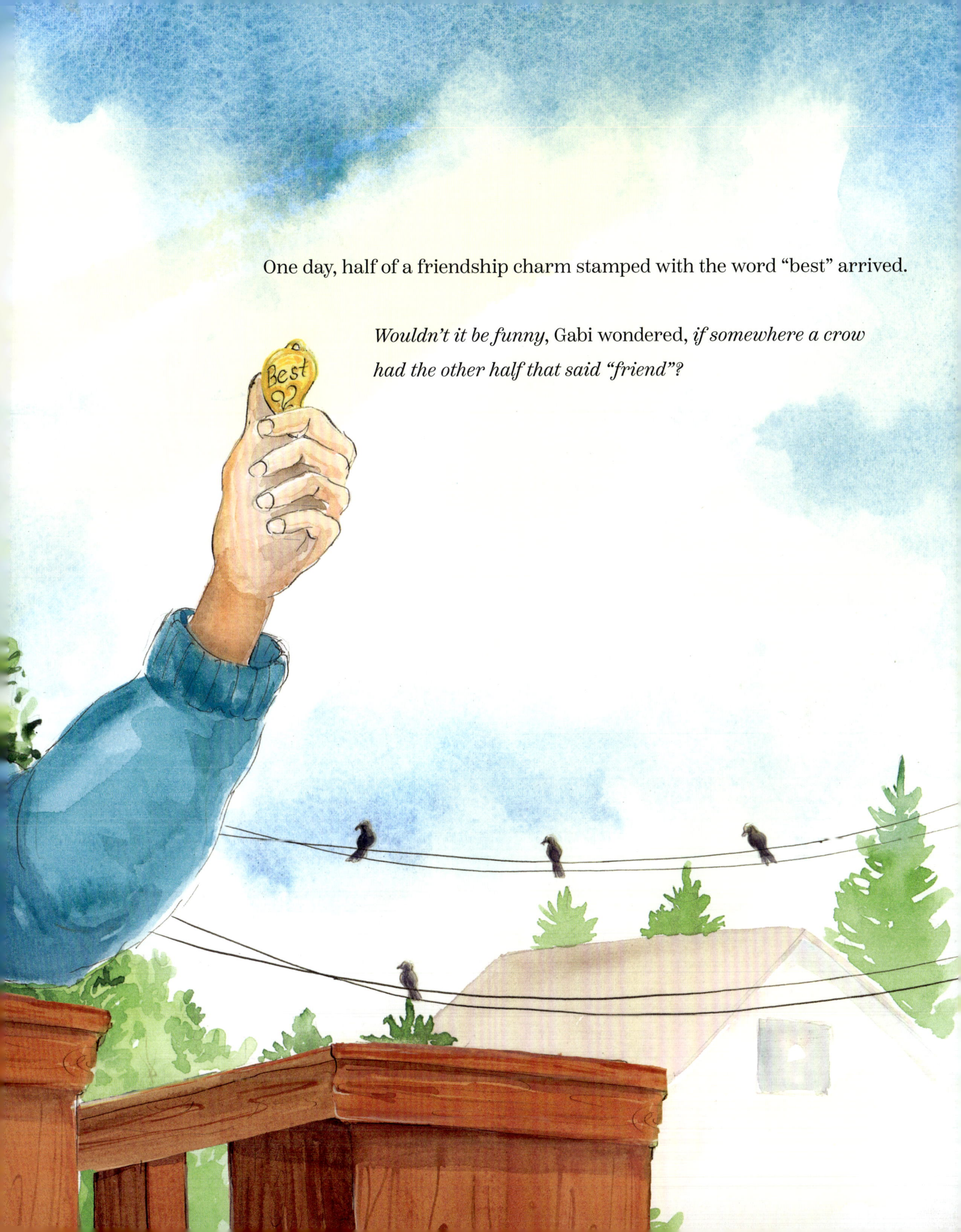

One day, half of a friendship charm stamped with the word “best” arrived.

Wouldn’t it be funny, Gabi wondered, *if somewhere a crow had the other half that said “friend”?*

Gabi's story might be the most well known, but friendships between humans and crows are more common than you'd think.

All around the world there are stories of friends who, together, go for
jogs
and hikes
and drives.

There are crows who eat breakfast at the table,
protect the family dog,
help garden,
play hide-and-seek,
and introduce their children,
so that all might be friends.
And of course, there are gifts!

Gifts of gratitude,

for friendship

and feeding,

or even being freed from a fence.

This morning, like so many before it, Gabi fed the crows.

This morning, like so many before it, their bond grew stronger.

All around the world, friendships flourished and flew.

So, what do you think?

Both givers of gifts and gifts to the world . . .

would you like to be friends with a crow?

Author's Note

When I was growing up—right about the age Gabi is in this book—my parents owned a little educational zoo, and my best friend was a Caique parrot named Kiwi. When I arrived in the mornings or after school, I would open the cage so that he could jump onto my shoulder and off we'd go to share the day. My friendship with Kiwi was as real and important as any I had with a human.

When I heard Gabi's story, I instantly felt a kinship and was in awe of her empathy and attitude toward crows. So often, and so mistakenly, we consider animals as below us or less important—but Gabi didn't. Led by curiosity and love, Gabi showed the world the wonders possible when humans treat animals with kindness. I hope Gabi's story is as inspirational to you as it was to me. There are millions of animals out there who would *love* to be your friend. Just treat them, especially wild animals, with respect and care.

Some of Gabi's gifts from crows

Thank you to Katy Sewall for expertly chronicling Gabi's story (see links in bibliography) and to Dr. Loma Pendergraf for fact-checking and reviewing this book.